Hope Wins

Hope Wins

We Can Change the World

Cathryn Wellner

Espoir Press
British Columbia
2014

Espoir Press
1002 – 1128 Sunset Drive
Kelowna, British Columbia
Canada V1Y 9W7

@2014 Cathryn Wellner; 2nd edition 2015
We borrow bits and pieces from all that our senses absorb.
We recombine them and call the result ours. Shakespeare
did it. So did Walt Disney. So do I. That recombining is our
original contribution to the world.

This is mine. I am grateful to the inspiring people who fill
my life with hope and to everyone who supports the
creative process by buying this book.

Library and Archives Canada Cataloging in Publication
Wellner, Cathryn
        Hope Wins: One story at a time

1. Hope. 2. Optimism. 3. Conduct of life. I. Title.

BF698.35.O57W45 2014 158   C2014-907943-5
                                C2014-907944-3

ISBN 978-0-9939623-0-1 (paperback)
ISBM 978-0-9939623-1-8 (e-book) (

All photographs by Cathryn Wellner
"A World Without Violence" by permission of Donna Milner
Quotes by Parker J. Palmer by permission of Mr. Palmer

For Robin Jarman, my best cheerleader,
and to friends, readers, and blog followers
who have encouraged me
to keep sharing reasons for hope.

"Hope" is the thing with feathers -
That perches in the soul -
And sings the tune without the words -
And never stops - at all -

And sweetest - in the Gale - is heard -
And sore must be the storm -
That could abash the little Bird
That kept so many warm -

I've heard it in the chillest land -
And on the strangest Sea -
Yet - never - in Extremity,
It asked a crumb - of me.

~ Emily Dickinson, 1861 (public domain)

Preface

According to today's news, I should be down in the dumps. Yet I will end the day on a high because I have an endless supply of a secretly intoxicating sauce: hope.

You are invited to enjoy all the secret sauce you can handle. When life tosses a lemon your way, turn it into lemonade. You will find good ingredients in these stories. Share them widely. When you do, people will tell you of other examples of rainbows suddenly appearing in a cloudy sky, of glimmers of light appearing in the proverbial tunnel.

If someone accuses you of being a Pollyanna because you embrace hope, remind them of the terrorist's son who chose compassion over hatred or of the people who rushed to help out a bus monitor who was the victim of bullying. Tell them to spend a week writing down both the bad things and good things that happen to them and to notice how even while we are in crisis, life hands us roses.

Choose the hope road. Detours and unexpected turns are normal. So are laughter and joy.

In 2011 the daily dose of bad news was getting me down. I figured if I could come up with 1,001 reasons for hope, I might be able to forge more of a shield. So I began a blog, This Gives Me Hope.

The number of followers grew. They re-posted entries on Facebook, Twitter, Stumble Upon and other social media. When I neared 1,001, they asked me to continue. By that time I had made a habit of looking for reasons for hope. Friends and readers were sending more ideas. I reached 1,001 and kept going.

This small book is the first of a new series that is growing out of the blog. The volumes that follow will gather hope-filled stories around such themes as aging, animals, the arts, youth, the environment, the search for meaning, education, different abilities, food, gender identity, business, technology, peace and politics. The stories are like bees. Instead of pollinating flowers, they pollinate hope.

The stories in this book, and the ones that follow, are for dreamers and schemers, visionaries and worriers, speakers and teachers and cockeyed optimists...and anyone else needing a quick dose of hope. They will help you build a habit of hope, a handful of stories at a time.

On the great balance scale of life, with the paralysis of despair on one side and the impetus of hope on the other, hope wins.

Contents

Starting a Hope-FULL Journey

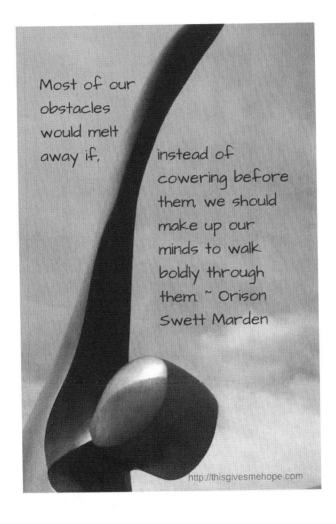

Most of our obstacles would melt away if, instead of cowering before them, we should make up our minds to walk boldly through them. ~ Orison Swett Marden

Take the Seeds of Life and Turn Them into Flowers

Some days our mistakes are so embarrassing they make us want to crawl into a cave. What Herbie Hancock learned from Miles Davis was how to turn those mistakes into something beautiful.

Hancock told the story in a CBC interview promoting his new book, *Possibilities*. It is one he tells often. He said he was touring with Davis. One night, the music was soaring, the audience enthralled, the performance building. Miles Davis was playing a solo, the others weaving their notes around his. Suddenly the young Hancock played a chord so out of synch with the rest he was sure he had just ruined the entire evening.

That is when Miles Davis taught Hancock the deep spirit of jazz. Hancock could hear the tiny pause as Davis internalized the unintended shift in the music. Drawing on his deep and broad knowledge of jazz, he played around Hancock's chord, turning something "wrong" into a shining detour.

3

That night Hancock understood jazz in a new way. He understood, in a way he had not before, that for jazz musicians there are no wrong notes, just notes to be explored and built on. What Hancock had seen as a concert-ruining misstep was just one more chance to grow something splendid out of the soil of a challenging chord.

Today, right now, you are enough. You do not have to be perfect to prove your worth. The mistakes of your life are seeds. Plant them in the fertile soil of your being and turn them into flowers.

What happens next is sheer magic. Someone catches sight of your vibrant petals, sniffs the fragrance of your blooming, and is inspired to plant her own seeds. On it goes, each flower showy enough in its own soil yet more brilliant in connection with those around.

That is when hope wins. The flowers of our lives grow from seeds planted in soil nourished by the compost of mistakes, tragedies and mishaps. Seen in the larger context of our lives, those missteps lose their poisonous power and enrich the soil that nourishes us and inspires others.

This little book is a celebration of life's seeds— sprouting, blooming, fading and creating more seeds of hope.

The Road Not Taken

Starting a hope-full journey does involve choosing which road to take. The news gives us plenty of reasons to figure the world is on a downhill slide. Beyond the headlines are the stories of kindness, generosity, compassion and courage. Those stories are about people who stand at a crossroads and choose hope.

Two roads diverged in a yellow wood,
And sorry I could not travel both
And be one traveler, long I stood
And looked down one as far as I could
To where it bent in the undergrowth;
Then took the other, as just as fair,
And having perhaps the better claim,
Because it was grassy and wanted wear;
Though as for that the passing there
Had worn them really about the same,
And both that morning equally lay
In leaves no step had trodden black.
Oh, I kept the first for another day!
Yet knowing how way leads on to way,
I doubted if I should ever come back.
I shall be telling this with a sigh

Somewhere ages and ages hence:
Two roads diverged in a wood, and I—
I took the one less traveled by,
And that has made all the difference.
    ~ Robert Frost, 1916 (public domain)

Be hopefully naïve

In Bill McKibben's January 2012 essay for YES!—"Why I'm Giving Up Cynicism for New Year's"—he made a distinction between two kinds of naivety, hopeless and hopeful. He preferred the latter, to be hopefully naïve.

That highlights the difference between optimism and hope. Optimism can be hopelessly naïve, insisting everything will be all right, no matter what. Hope takes a clear-eyed look at the way things are and chooses to love the world anyway. Hope gets things done even if optimism tumbles into despondency.

Governments around the globe slide toward the right. Multinational corporations wield unprecedented power. The environment strains under the weight of our carelessness.

And yet... People erect little libraries on posts and stock them with books they want to share. In Moab, Utah, ten percent of the town's 5,000 people turn out for the 2011 Gay Pride parade. Photographer Jen McKen takes a stand against bullying by refusing to take graduation pictures of girls posting cruel comments on Facebook. And on it goes.

Giving in to despair, believing the world and its people are irredeemably at risk, overlooks some major shifts that have taken place just in my lifetime. In much of the world, smoking in public spaces is no longer considered acceptable. Many young people are foregoing car ownership and opting for more environmentally sensitive lifestyles. People with gender orientations outside heterosexist "norms" can increasingly express their love without fear of reprisal. Those are big shifts.

We are not condemned to accept the way things are. We can bring about change, and each one of us can make a difference.

We Can All Soar

When I began blogging 1,001 reasons for hope in May 2011, the task seemed overwhelming. Then I found a dozen, a hundred, hundreds of reasons. Inspiration rolled in from people around the world. They introduced me to:

- Julius Mwelu, the photographer who puts cameras in the hands of youth living in slums and lets them tell the powerful stories of the people around them
- Claude Demarais, the professor who dreamed Preservation Farm into existence
- Mary Johnson, who found it in heart to forgive her son's killer
- Our Time Theatre, where only stutterers can participate and where they thrive on unconditional love
- Aunty Grace Dick and Joan Rayment, whose cross-cultural friendship spans 50 years and thousands of miles
- The good people at The Little Free Library, who build tiny libraries, attach them to posts

> and encourage people to plant them in neighborhoods everywhere
>
> - Roscoe, the dog who adopted a neighborhood and who is loved and fiercely protected by the people there

They taught me that everyone harbors the seeds of greatness, whether our gift is photography, farming or friendship.

We all get discouraged. Sometimes we feel small and inadequate. That is where *Hope Wins* comes in. When life hands you lemons, take a few minutes to read a hope-filled story or two. Add them to speeches. Share them with students and friends. They will give you the inspiration you need to spread your wings and soar.

Hope Costs Nothing But Changes Everything

We watch the news and drop into a pit of despair. Some of us dismiss hope as the cotton candy of simplistic fools, sweet on the tongue but without substance. But those who smell the rose of hope in the swamp of worry possess a treasure. Anyone can have it, and it doesn't cost a thing.

For those needing scientific underpinning for something as seemingly intangible as hope, Anthony Scioli and Henry Biller offer help. Both are professors of psychology, Dr. Scioli at Keene State College in New Hampshire and Dr. Biller at the University of Rhode Island. Their research has uncovered "a place for hope in the age of anxiety".

In their book, *The Power of Hope*, they call hope a middle ground between becoming caught in a maelstrom of stress and anxiety on the one hand and giving up completely on the other.

The payoff for cultivating a hope habit, according to Scioli and Biller, can include better health, self-confidence, and resilience. Everyone rides life's roller coaster. As it races down into an inevitable trough, hopeful people anticipate the next peak.

Reading the "Hope Lessons" on their Gain Hope website, I am reminded of the old story of a man who was working on a construction site. Someone stopped to ask what he was doing. "I'm building a cathedral," he said.

That is a hopeful mindset. He was not just carrying stones or hammering nails or some other small task. He was part of something larger. What's more, he knew his part was important.

That is hope.

For Good Health, Cultivate Hope

One of the curious things about this hope journey is coming across people convinced the world is going to hell in a hand basket and there is precious little we can do about it. Anyone who has followed This Gives Me Hope for a while or dug around in the entries will know I have no illusions about life's being all sweetness and light. But I believe that goodness is far more prevalent than evil. I am too busy giving credit to compassionate change makers to wallow in hopelessness or cynicism.

I may live a longer, healthier life because of my decision to focus on hope. A study published in the *Journal of the American Academy of Neurology* found that cynical people were more at risk for dementia. They acknowledged the dementia link was preliminary, but it was an intriguing finding.

A 2007 study reported in the *Journal of the American Medical Association* linked cardiovascular disease with cynical distrust, hostility, chronic stress and depression. The earlier study had about five times as many participants (6,814 versus 1,449) and also linked cynicism with unhealthy behaviours (*e.g.,* obesity and smoking) that contribute to heart disease.

Even further back, 1993, a team of researchers publishing in *Epidemiology* found a link between hopelessness and heart disease. Women, blacks, unmarried people, smokers, and those physically inactive or less educated were more likely to experience hopelessness.

Scientists are cautious about mixing up correlation and causation. Still, these and other studies keep drawing a connection between our health and our attitudes.

Just in case they are right, keep looking for the true, the good and the beautiful. We cannot cheat death and decay, but the ride to the grave might as well be fun. And you just might have more years of health, which sounds like a big hope bonus.

Listen for the Right Notes

During the years I taught storytelling workshops, students kept asking me to be hard on them. They wanted me to ferret out every small failing in their delivery, every tiny stumble in their stories. I was not comfortable with that. I wanted to point out what was right with their storytelling so they would do more of it.

I had believed for a long time that we influence the world by what we focus on. It made sense to me that if I emphasized my students' weaknesses, they would repeat them next time. On the other hand, if I told them where their storytelling was strongest, they would look for ways to bring those elements into their telling. Besides, like everyone else, I had experienced my share of painful barbs from people wanting to improve me. I had no wish to become someone else's bad memory.

Then I read the story of Pablo Casals and a young cellist. It was one of those pivotal moments when something we hear or read or see affects us so profoundly we never forget it.

The gist of the story is this: A young cellist had the opportunity to play for the master. He tackled a particularly difficult piece and made many mistakes.

15

He was mortified when the great Casals praised his playing. In fact, he was disappointed his idol did not rip apart what was so obviously a flawed performance. The incident haunted him.

Years later the young man met Casals again. By then he had established a successful career and wondered if Casals remembered hearing him so long before. Casals did remember so the young man asked why he had praised such an error-filled performance. Casals sat down at his cello, picked up his bow and began the piece he had heard the young musician play years before.

"Didn't you play it this way?" he asked.

The young man nodded, and Casals played another passage. "And isn't this the way you played this section?"

Again the young man nodded.

"I had never thought of playing it that way," said Casals, expressing gratitude for the younger man's originality.

What Pablo Casals taught the young cellist is that anyone can hear the wrong notes. It takes a musician to hear what is right, what is unusual, what is inspired.

That story has stayed with me for more than three decades. It has guided me as a storyteller, a teacher, a community developer, and a writer. It is still the shining star I walk toward as I write about reasons for hope.

Anyone can hear the wrong notes. Our task is to look for what is right.

Turning Humiliation into Hope

This is probably going to sound strange, but the response to a horrifying YouTube video gives me hope. The bare details are: Karen Huff Klein was still working at the age of 68. She was a bus monitor in a school district I used to work for, the Greece School District just north of Rochester, New York. Her job was to make sure students got on and off the bus with no problems and were safe en route.

A few days before the school year ended, four middle-school students decided to have a bit of fun with her. Their idea of fun was to belittle and swear at her, to threaten and demean.

For ten horrible minutes, they filmed their bit of fun. Then they posted the video on YouTube.

Here's where the hope comes in. Max Sidorov, a Toronto blogger, was appalled when he watched the video. He launched an Indiegogo campaign to let Karen Huff Klein know that people cared about what happened to her and that they wanted to do something nice for her.

He hoped to raise $5000 so she could take a nice vacation, something she could never afford on her salary of $15,506. He never dreamed so many people would chip in. When the campaign ended, a total of $703,873 had been raised.

Klein went on that holiday. The money allowed her to retire and launch an anti-bullying campaign. It was as if Karen Huff Klein had won the lottery. Unfortunately, the winning ticket was dreadful and inflicted a wound that will leave a scar.

So why did the incident give me hope? Because so many good people stepped up so quickly. Because people around the world wanted something good to come out of what Klein had endured. Because the message everyone gave to the young bullies was: This kind of brutality will not be allowed.

One, awful event and its encouraging aftermath will not stop the violence people do to each other's bodies and spirits. Still, in this one case, strangers drew a circle of love around a victim and a circle of disapproval around the bullies.

It was only one step, but it was one step. And that is how the journey to compassion begins.

Moin Khan, Motorcyclist for Peace

Whatever hope-filled path you choose, start with what you love most. That is what Moin Khan did.

Khan was five when he saw his first heavy motorcycle and went crazy for it. But the Lahore-born Pakistani Muslim did not have a chance to act on his passion until he went to the United States for university in 2005. Along with learning how to operate a motorcycle, he learned that many Americans saw people like him as bomb-building terrorists. He decided to do something to try to change people's perceptions of his country.

After graduating from San Francisco State University with a degree in international business, he worked three jobs and saved every extra penny to fund a motorcycle trip from San Francisco to Lahore. He set out with no maps or GPS, happy to get lost many times a day since that gave him the chance to meet someone new each time he had to ask directions.

His route took him north into Canada, across the Prairie provinces, south around the Great Lakes, across the Atlantic to Europe, along a meandering route that finally ended in Lahore.

The trip was hazardous. An accident in Romania nearly ended the dream. He broke three ribs, a shoulder, a wrist and a finger. His recovery was more than physical. People from around the world sent him parts to repair his motorcycle, signing them with positive messages. A Romanian mechanic showed up to do the repairs. The hospital gave him free care. His father encouraged him to continue.

And so he did. Moin Khan was given a hero's welcome when he finally reached Lahore on December 31, 2011, after six months on the road. After seeing so much of the world, he had a new dream and started a school where girls could learn to drive motorcycles. He wanted Pakistani women to experience the freedom they have in other parts of the world.

Moin Khan has raised funds to donate warm clothing to Pakistanis in cold regions, distributing hundreds of hoodies, blankets, warm socks and beanies. In 2013 he led two riders on a trip around Pakistan. In 2014 a total of fourteen riders joined him on two different trips.

The second 2014 trip, with nine Americans (two female andseven male). Brighto Paints sponsored it and sent a crew to capture the adventure. Khan's dream was to share the beauty of the country and perhaps inspire others to lead adventures there.

Wherever he shows the documentary, audiences are awed by the drama of the landscape the riders drove through. Even more important, they find their preconceptions challenged. The motorcyclists who set out on this adventure with Khan experienced hospitality and stunning vistas, connecting the spirits of visitors with a Pakistan they might otherwise never have known. Any who experience these tours will return home transformed.

Khan has become a one-man peace mission, gathering friends wherever he travels, opening people's eyes to the beauty to be found in the hearts of strangers.

Where will you start your journey of hope?

A World Without Violence

There is no 'us' or 'them'

There is only We
We are one
We are whole
We are the people of the world

And we the Children of the world
Play in our yards, our fields, our streets and parks
Alone, safe, unafraid,
And the only cries you hear
Are cries of laughter as we
Play tag under the street lamps at dusk
Or hide-and-seek in the dark of an autumn night
While the innocent wind whispers in the drying
        leaves
And the voices of our mothers and fathers call us
        home to dinner.

And We the women of the world
Are free to choose our own path through life

And if that path should take…
A Korean student down a jogging trail by Lost
    Lagoon in Stanley Park,
A middle-aged mother on her bicycle down a quiet
    country road in the Cariboo,
A First Nations daughter, sister, friend, down the
    darkened streets of East Vancouver,
Or a young woman in Coquitlam to the corner bus
    stop in the early morning mist,
She goes without fear of attack, without fear of the
    dark,
For there is no evil lurking in the shadows
And the only difference between day and night is the
    degree of light.
And We the Men of the world
Stand beside you under the same sun, the same
    moon, the same stars
And if we should put our arms around you there in
    the darkness
It is with love… and agreement.
We are the people of the world
All nations, colours, races, religions and creeds
We do no harm to one another with weapons or
    with words
Because we could not bear the pain.
We are connected,
We are one.
We have no locks, no gates, no borders,
In our homes, our communities, our world,
There is no violence.

There is only Peace.

Pray for it

©2003 Donna Milner

Donna Milner wrote this for a production of The Vagina Monologues in Williams Lake, British Columbia. It still gives me shivers to read it. Donna's novels are spellbinding, peopled with characters you will recognize and love. They include *The Promise of Rain*, *After River* and *Somewhere In-Between*.

Hope Has Champions

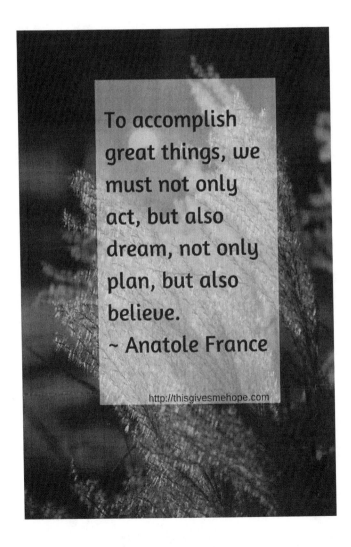

To accomplish great things, we must not only act, but also dream, not only plan, but also believe.

~ Anatole France

They Show Up When We Need Them

I am amazed every time it happens, even though it happens a lot. Sometimes they arrive in human form. Other times they appear as books or poems or paintings or birds flying overhead. They are signposts, though we may not understand what they were telling us until much later. They are hope's champions, pointing us toward the next steps on our journey through life.

In this section you will meet some of those champions. They do not necessarily identify themselves that way, but they shine their light on the path we all seek, the one that leads to a well-lived and satisfying life.

Before you read about them, meet three of my own special champions. Jay O'Callahan entered my life when I was moving from Rochester, New York, to Seattle, Washington. I was burning with the desire to throw myself into storytelling full time. Jay was a star in the storytelling world. He was one of the presenters at a conference. I took every opportunity to tell my handful of stories when he was in the audience.

At one point he asked my plans for the move to Seattle. I mumbled something about not being sure, and he gave me a gift. "You could always tell stories," he said. I tucked that talisman in my heart. When I arrived in

Seattle, I declared myself a storyteller and carved out a niche for myself.

Patti Digh was another of my champions. I have never met Patti, but when I picked up *Life Is a Verb: 37 Days to Wake Up, Be Mindful, and Live Intentionally* in a Seattle book store, I knew I had found a kindred spirit. I loved the easy flow, the informality, the honesty of her words. At the time, a friend and I were planning to write a book together. I showed her Patti's book and said, "This is it! This is what our book is going to look like. This is the design I've been trying to describe to you."

My friend's complicated life shifted directions for both of us. The book had to be shelved, but I still return to my marked-up copy of Patti's book for inspiration. She began that book as a blog, which encouraged me to start my own. That was a life-changing decision. This book is one of the results.

The third was a poet. When my life was foundering on the broken shards of a second marriage, and I figured I'd used up my life's supply of good-girl points, I read and re-read Mary Oliver's poem, "Wild Geese", from *Dream Work*. I cried every time, but her words reminded me I did not have to be perfect, not even good, to earn my place on the planet.

I have moved repeatedly since then and given away possessions each time. But when I have opened boxes in my new home, Oliver's books are always there.

Champions of hope show up when our hearts are open to them. They may be the lines of a song, the encouragement of a friend, the sudden moments of grace. They do not solve our problems or make our lives perfect, but they reassure us we have turned a corner. We know, once again, we will be all right.

A Rope to the Barn for Souls Caught in a Blizzard

Parker J. Palmer's interview with Alicia von Stamwitz came onto my Facebook timeline and went straight into my heart. The night before, I had explained to friends that I began the hope blog when I felt the hopelessness of daily news sinking into my bones. I decided if I wanted to see the world in a brighter light, I had to start with myself. I had to spend more time looking at what was right with the world.

Von Stamwitz interviewed Palmer about the book he had just published, *Healing the Heart of Democracy: The Courage to Create a Politics Worthy of the Human Spirit*. When she asked about the genesis of the book, he told her:

> *"I started writing it in 2004 or 2005 because I was in a psychological hole. I was in a lot of despair myself about what was happening in our country, about our inability to talk to each other, about democracy going down the tubes. And it was actually a period of depression for me. Part of my journey involves three major experiences with clinical depression, and one of the things I learned in my*

previous bouts was that if you get a little bit of energy, you have to do something proactive related to what's causing the depression. Becoming proactive can be therapeutic, can be life-giving. So I started writing this book. I basically argue that what we call the politics of rage [in the United States], if you look at it more deeply, is in fact the politics of the brokenhearted. I believe that there's heartbreak across the political spectrum, all the way to the radical ends."

I read the interview just after another shooting spree in the U.S., this time in a Maryland shopping mall. Parker told von Stamwitz violence is the result of people's not knowing what to do with their suffering. He said nations do that too, as America did after 9/11, manipulating fear to justify more violence. We see the same phenomenon on large and small scales, all around the globe.

Yet hope is not a luxury; it is a necessity. Parker J. Palmer offers a vivid metaphor. In his book, *A Hidden Wholeness*, Palmer describes our despair at the storm of violence, environmental degradation or economic injustice as being lost in a blizzard, fearing we have irretrievably lost our way. Then he adds a lifeline:

"But my own experience of the blizzard, which includes getting lost in it more often than I like to admit, tells me that it is not so. The soul's order can never be destroyed. It may be obscured by the whiteout. We may forget, or deny, that its guidance is close at hand. And yet we are still in the soul's backyard, with chance after chance to regain our bearings.

31

> *"This book is about tying a rope from the back door out to the barn so that we can find our way home again. When we catch sight of the soul, we can survive the blizzard without losing our hope or our way. When we catch sight of the soul, we can become healers in a wounded world—in the family, in the neighborhood, in the workplace, and in political life—as we are called back to our "hidden wholeness" amid the violence of the storm."*

Palmer's metaphor perfectly describes *Hope Wins*. It is a rope to the barn door of hope. No matter what may happen in your life or the world around you, you can find your way home again.

If you awaken to bad news, if life feels out of control, if you are lost in the storm, grab hold of the rope at any point. Hang onto it, and find your way back home.

Figure Out What You Hope For

Hope is on my mind a lot these days and not just because I am on a daily search for reasons to be hopeful. Friends are facing challenges that make hope seem like a shiny bauble on a Christmas tree— pretty but perhaps not relevant. And that doesn't take into account all the horrors being perpetrated around the globe.

The seduction of despair is real, but it is not useful. Barbara Kingsolver reminded us in *Animal Dreams*, that figuring out what we hope for is an important part of our life's work. She built on that in her 2008 commencement address at Duke University. She reminded the graduating students that we have done the seemingly impossible in the past. Americans ended slavery, in spite of arguments the economy would collapse without it. Women in most countries around the world can vote, own property and make decisions about their lives.

Everyone has heard the story of the Christmas truce in World War I, when German and American soldiers climbed out of their trenches, sang, shared treats and, for a precious few hours, stopped the killing. Decades later, when air traffic was halted because of the terrible events of September 11, 2001, the good people of Gander, Newfoundland, opened their homes and hearts to thousands of stranded passengers.

The truth is, good people are everywhere, and there are far more of them than of those who cause us so much despair. Perfection is not something any of us will acquire in our lifetimes, but along our journey we can offer to the world as much goodness as we can muster.

Hope can triumph over despair. It is not the smooth path. It is a road with many barriers and boulders. We are tempted to detour or turn back. But detours present new challenges, and turning back means facing the hurdles we already navigated.

The only sane path through life is to hang onto hope.

Hope Is No Sissy

This hope journey is the best I have ever been on. So a passage from Rob Bell's *Velvet Elvis: Repainting The Christian Faith* leaped out at me. He wrote that hope is our gift to the world. He was not talking about the kind of hope that paints everything a rosy hue. He meant the kind that is tempered like steel, by walking through and surviving the fire of suffering we all endure in one way or another. Hope is strong and defiant in the face of pain. It refuses to accept as final whatever we are enduring.

That is why I have written about Talia, the feisty cancer patient, and Kasha Jacqueline Nabagesera, fierce fighter for LGBT justice in Uganda. It is why people like Bob Quinn, the scrappy advocate for addicts, and the fierce grandmothers who demonstrate against injustice, give me hope.

People like Rob Bell give me hope too. I had never read anything by the popular and controversial minister and was curious about him. Lydia Schoch, Twitter friend and talented blogger suggested I read *Velvet Elvis*. The book was a good introduction. I can see why he is popular among Christians who feel crowded out by right-wing evangelism and guilt-inducing dogma. To me he sounds like a Unitarian Universalist with a Christian bent.

That landed Bell in hot water in some circles, especially after he published his 2011 book, *Love Wins: A Book About Heaven, Hell, and the Fate of Every Person Who Ever Lived*. When he dismissed the concept of eternal damnation, he angered a lot of followers in the mega church he had founded. He ended up having to leave the Mars Hill congregation. On the other hand, when he embraced a loving, rather than punitive, God he likely attracted others, people who figure if there is an afterlife, Christians will have to share it with saints and reprobates and people of every possible religious stripe.

Bell's concept of hope is not something naive and puny. It is intelligent and clear eyed. Hope is not about everyone's arriving at the same destination and living happily ever after. It is about being signposts for each other, using our own experiences to point toward the next stage of the journey for someone else.

Street Books, a Library for Portland's Homeless

"Read any good books lately?" would probably not be a conversation opener for most people passing a homeless person on the street. For the Street Books librarians, it would be a perfectly normal interaction.

The bicycle-powered library started in Portland, Oregon, in 2011 when Laura Moulton was given a three-month grant to establish a mobile library. As she told Rebecca Koffman for *The Oregonian*, she knew by summer's end the project had to continue. Arriving late for one of the final shifts of the project, she found Keith waiting for her. Disappointing him by not providing any more books was not an option.

Street Books is now a non-profit organization, and it still delivers the books. Three days a week, three different librarians peddle the library to different locations around Portland. During their three-hour shifts, homeless readers borrow and return books and chat with other book lovers. No library card or permanent address is required. Street Books is thrilled when people return the books but not upset when they don't.

The Street Books Web site displays photographs and book reviews of people who want to share their experiences. The results shatter stereotypes about people who find themselves living on the street. I scrolled through the stories and pictures with a lump in my throat.

The attractive little library does something else that is important and beautiful. It breaks down walls between those who are homeless and those not sure how to interact with street people.

Diane Rempe, a community psychologist and Street Books volunteer, told Koffman that providing books for people living on the streets was "nourishment of other sorts". Books go beyond the basic services of food, shelter and health care, acknowledging that the mind needs stimulation, whatever our circumstances.

Street Books is an idea that could work in any community. It is what Ben Hodgson, a Street Books user who is now back on his feet, calls "one of those tender mercies".

Hope Is the Heart of Prosperity

It never occurred to me to see hope as the heart of prosperity until Tim Jackson pointed out that "prosperity" holds within it the Old French verb for "to hope". That is profound and important.

Growing up in a single-parent family, on a down-in-the-heels, dead-end street in Twin Falls, Idaho, I always had hope. It was as close as knowing I would never go to bed hungry and as distant as my dreams of growing up to make a difference in the world.

Hope is elusive for many. It can be hard to hang onto for the malnourished child of a smallholder displaced by a multinational corporation, for the girl forbidden the chance to go to school and forced into an early marriage, for the unemployed worker whose company sent his job to a factory overseas, for the Pacific Islander losing her home to climate change or for the Palestinian without a homeland.

In part, hope is a function of economic opportunity. Yet the view of economics as the promise of endless growth offers no solutions for the suffering of the world nor the gasping of the planet. We are told we must choose between jobs and the environment, as if there were no other path. We watch the news, believe violence and loss are inevitable, and lose heart.

Fortunately, there are other ways. Tim Jackson, Professor of Sustainable Development at the UK's University of Surrey, is an articulate proponent of one promising path, that of sustainable consumption. He quotes Mary Douglas, from an essay on poverty written nearly four decades ago: "What is the objective of the consumer? It is to help create the social world and find a credible place in it."

As Jackson says in a TED talk, we crave novelty. That makes us the manufacturer's dream. Offer us a new smartphone, and we ditch the old, though it still meets our needs. Jackson reminds us we have nobler qualities. We are more than our consumer drives. Our minds and spirits are fertile ground in which we can plant the seeds of creativity, learning, spirituality, compassion, generosity, and so much more.

We can turn those nobler qualities toward solving many of the problems we have created. We can devise industrial processes that are kinder to the environment, social systems that narrow the enormous inequalities that leave so many people in poverty, and health services more responsive to the context of our lives.

We see examples of companies that focus on social and ecological goals and cities that provide shared spaces such as libraries, community gardens, parks, museums, walking paths, and skating rinks. They connect us to community, providing spaces where all are welcome.

Jackson does not espouse eliminating capitalism or changing our human nature. He does, in reminding us that the word "prosperity" incorporates hope, urge us to see economics as a malleable human system. Our insistence on endless growth as the only path to prosperity is too costly to people and planet.

Jackson believes sustainable development is not only essential. It is also possible. That is a hope-filled vision.

Turn the Planet
Toward Life

I n 1971 a bestseller landed on my book shelf. With its
spiral binding, *Diet for a Small Planet* was easy to prop
open on a kitchen counter, while this novice cook
learned how to create healthy meals.

The author was 26-year-old Frances Moore Lappé.
She was ahead of her time in calling for a vegetarian diet
as a way of safeguarding the planet. In the years since
then, she has authored seventeen more books, founded
several national organizations and worked tirelessly on
behalf of the environment and social justice.

By the time she published *Hope's Edge* in 2002, I was
farming organically and deeply involved in food systems
issues. Like the earliest book, this one had a profound
impact on me, inspiring me to believe the global food
system could be sustainable and just, in spite of the
problems I was working to address.

Her daughter would have cut her eye teeth on social
activism so it is no surprise Anna Lappé joined her
mother to launch the Small Planet Institute, whose
slogan is "Living democracy, feeding hope."

The first sentence of their mission articulates a
simple, profound argument for hope: "We believe that

ideas have enormous power and that humans are capable of changing failing ideas in order to turn our planet toward life."

In a June 2013 conversation with Fritjof Capra for the Center for Ecoliteracy, Frances Moore Lappé confirmed her belief, saying, "Hope is what we become in action together in community."

Her latest book, *EcoMind: Changing the Way We Think, to Create the World We Want,* is a call to turn away from fear and toward possibility. She presents a vision that is buoyantly hopeful, where the systems we humans have created are redesigned in ways that make our cities sustainable and resilient.

That shift in thinking throws off the shackles of uncertainty and negativity and opens wide the doors of connection, with each other, with other species, and with the earth. It is a hope-filled vision.

Warrior of Hope

For any who fear hope is a wimp, that it is the white flag of surrender raised above the messy fray of real life, meet Chris Hedges, warrior of hope.

Born in 1956, Chris Hedges is a journalist whose writing focuses on American politics and society. For years he was a foreign correspondent for major news media. Son of a Presbyterian minister, he speaks out for what he believes, whatever the cost. He is an equal-opportunity critic, castigating left, right and center in the interests of social justice.

In 2010 Chris Hedges joined war veterans in civil disobedience that landed him in jail. The veterans and their supporters, and Chris Hedges, anticipated they would be arrested for their action. But they were warriors of hope, and warriors of hope are willing to take risks.

In a talk before his arrest, he warned those gathered that peace comes at a cost. He said hope is not the easy road. It is the path of action. But along with the risks come the possibilities for transforming ourselves and others.

Chris Hedges has called nonviolent civil disobedience "our only hope". Given the willingness of governments and corporations to destroy the planet while distracting us with platitudes, he may be right. We are a scrappy and peculiar species, embracing a consumerism we know is hastening the destruction of the environment that sustains us.

We are also a species capable of kindness, astonishing intelligence, compassion and innovation. Chris Hedges reminds us to fulfill our potential rather than settle for mediocrity.

Son of a terrorist chose tolerance and empathy

Zak Ebrahim was brought up on a diet of hate. He was 10 when his father, the notorious Egyptian-American, El Sayyid-Nosair, shot Rabbi Meir Kehane in 1990. He was 13 when his father, from his prison cell, helped plan the 1993 bombing of the World Trade Center. The beloved, gentle father changed from a middle-class engineer into a radical jihadist after he fell in with a group of fundamentalist Muslims.

Ebrahim's mother divorced Nosair but married a man who turned out to be just as radical and hate-filled. Even worse for the family, the stepfather proved to be violent and abusive.

Ebrahim and his family spent most of his childhood on the move. They changed their names to hide their relationship to El Sayyid-Nosair. Even without that identity to mark him, as the new, chubby kid in the classroom, Ebrahim was the target of bullies at school and of bigotry at home.

He told a TED2014 audience he began to turn away from his father's teachings when in 2000 he participated in the National Youth Convention. As part of a group focusing on youth violence, he befriended a young man he discovered was Jewish. Another turning point was meeting people of different faiths and cultures during a summer working at Busch Gardens. Among the performers were young gays he found to be open and non-judgmental. Also, watching Jon Stewart, a Jewish comedian, opened his mind to his own bigotry.

He decided to go public with his real identity in order to challenge the radical hatred of people like his father. In his book, *The Terrorist's Son: A Story of Choice*, he tells the story of his father's embracing terrorism and what it was like to grow up in that shadow. In spite of being fed a diet of fanaticism and hatred, Ebrahim chose his own path. He opened his mind and heart to those his father despised.

Going public with a story like this requires considerable courage. We do not hear a lot about the families of terrorists. Like others, they marry, have children, and pass on their values. Ebrahim chose to strike out in a direction diametrically opposed to his father's. His blood ties with those widely feared for their fanaticism and violence make that decision far more momentous than most young people face.

In spite of the potential danger he faced in going public, Ebrahim chose to share his journey from bigotry to tolerance, from hatred to peace. He made a brave choice. He gives me hope.

Harry Potter Alliance Mobilizes Fans

During the years J.K. Rowling was churning out Harry Potter books, young fans carried around thick tomes and waited at the doors of their favorite book stores for the next installment. As a former librarian, I was thrilled by the enthusiasm of young readers.

Rowling ended the series and moved on to adult fiction. The Harry Potter Alliance moved on to changing the world. According to their mission statement, they use parallels from the books to inspire young people to get involved with issues of literacy, equality and human rights. While doing their part to make the world a better place, the young activists can envision themselves as heroes of the ilk found in J.K. Rowling's characters.

With so much competition for the attention of youth, linking social action with popular culture is a good idea. The Harry Potter Alliance harnesses the power of entertainment to galvanize action.

Andrew Slack created the alliance in 2009 and is its Executive Director. Using the lead character as inspiration, he formed an organization that gives participants a sense of their own power as advocates for social justice. Slack sees within Harry Potter fans a mighty force for good, each carrying the seeds of a better world. They are a Dumbledore's Army, waking the world and putting their energies toward ending the wrenching issues of our time.

A November 2013 article in YES! listed "8 courageous things Harry Potter fans did to fight real-life dark forces." Among them were disaster relief in Haiti, books for kids in Rwanda, and advocacy for immigration and marriage equality.

Their list of success stories is inspiring, as these examples show. They spurred Harry Potter Fans to pressure Warner Brothers to be transparent about their cocoa sources. Since the company was licensed to produce Harry Potter-brand chocolates, the campaign was appropriately titled, "Not In Harry's Name". An annual Accio Books initiative has supported literacy in Rwanda's Agahozo Shalom Youth Village through donations of tens of thousands of books and assistance with building libraries. In another effort they launched Odds in Our Favor, drawing on the dark messages of the Hunger Games to draw attention to economic inequality.

Even if the Harry Potter series stops being so popular among young people, the alliance is showing how to use cultural icons to inspire action. With 275 chapters in 25 countries and 43 U.S. states, the mighty army is expanding around the globe, determined to be a force for good.

Choosing nonviolence

The idea is simple. Shift our focus to what we want instead of what we fear. Give center stage to peace rather than war. Julia Bacha calls on media to do just that. She asks them to put peace in the spotlight instead of focusing nearly all of their attention on violence. In her talk for TED, Bacha uses the example of the Palestinian village of Budrus to make a compelling case.

For ten months in 2003, villagers staged a nonviolent protest, objecting to Israeli plans to construct a barrier across their olive groves. The barrier would have robbed them of 40 percent of their land. They would have been effectively imprisoned, with no free access to the rest of the West Bank. Day after day they marched and chanted and refused to respond to police provocation.

Israeli police shot live bullets in the air. They clubbed some of the demonstrators, both men and women. Instead of fighting back, the protestors responded with peaceful determination. Ten months later the Israeli government agreed to their demands.

Had Bacha not filmed the peaceful protests, they would have been almost completely ignored by media. Bacha observes that both violent and nonviolent resistance need an audience to be effective. In reporting conflict between Israel and Palestine, only violence attracts the headlines. That makes it harder for those leading peaceful protest to persuade community members they can be effective in their opposition to injustices.

By recording those refusing to respond to violence with retaliation, Bacha can prove that peaceful protest actually does work.

Now when Bacha shows her film to other villagers in the region, they are inspired to try peaceful protest rather than violence. Allies in the Israeli peace movement, Solidariot, use the film as a recruiting tool. Peace begets peace, yet most media ignore it.

So let's add our voices to Julia Bacha's. Together, we can pressure major media to draw attention to peaceful protest, to nonviolent demonstrations, and to the good and caring people of the world. Let's persuade them to replace their attachment to violence with a new focus on cooperation and peace.

Jews and Arabs Refusing to Be Enemies

How would the Arab-Israeli conflict change if Jews and Arabs just refused to be enemies? A Facebook page (Jews & Arabs Refuse To Be Enemies) is trying to find out.

That peace is elusive is no surprise, given the history of the region and the militancy on both sides. And no one is naive enough to expect a Facebook page and some demonstrations to eliminate enmity with such deep roots.

On the other hand, revolutions have brought down governments. Trying to topple entrenched positions through refusing to hate is a form of nonviolent, positive revolution. It begins at the grassroots level and ripples through ramparts of hostility.

The Facebook page was started by two Hunter College students, Abraham Gutman and Dania Garwish. Gutman told *Huffington Post* they had grown tired of all the hate on social media. They wanted to take a stand against hatred and intolerance by focusing on commonalities among supposed enemies. So they launched the Facebook page to provide a forum for Arabs and Israelis who were refusing to be enemies.

On both Facebook and Twitter (with the hashtag #JewsAndArabsRefuseToBeEnemies), people from around the world began posting pleas for peace. Some held signs declaring their refusal to hate or calling for tolerance and understanding. Others called for an end to violence. Couples, an Arab man and Jewish woman or the reverse, posted pictures of themselves embracing or kissing.

They posted articles and photographs detailing the deaths of those caught in the war in Gaza, of those displaced, of people from around the world showing support.

All of them were refusing to buy into sectarian extremism. They had no illusions a Facebook page would change the minority who espouse intransigence and hostility, but they hoped to raise awareness that far more people wish for peace and justice than for violence.

As tensions temporarily eased in the region, activity on the page let up, but it did not stop. So the page will be there as a reminder, and it will be there as a place for people to connect as people, not foes.

Peace is always worth a try, and it is always founded on hope.

Dancing for Joy, Dancing for Peace

Matt Harding was a videogame developer when he decided to take time out and travel the world. What made him an Internet sensation was his decision to film himself doing a silly dance at every stop. "Where the Hell Is Matt?" went viral, and he ended up making a second and a third video, all of them receiving millions of views.

In the first film, in 2006, he danced in front of iconic tourist spots. For his 2008 film he persuaded people to do his crazy dance with him.

For the 2012 film he had two new ideas. They showed a deeper understanding of how his work touched people. This time, he told an Italian interviewer, he tried different dances in each location and he went to places he couldn't before, such as Afghanistan, North Korea and Iraq, "places," he said, "that are often thought of as dangerous or unfriendly."

The 2012 dance video joined hands across barriers of culture, gender, age, and the incomprehension that settles in when we don't know each other's stories. On his Web site, Harding encouraged people to donate to seven organizations who helped him make it.

I smiled through his other videos, but the last one really touched my heart. I had a lump in my throat along with a silly grin on my face – until the last scene. When I saw Matt Harding dancing with his wife and baby, I cried.

So I wandered over to his blog (aka "Journal"). On June 25th there was a touching photograph of Harding watching the 2012 video with his son and Joel Davis's two boys. Davis called it "the single best baby pacifier known to man."

Music for the 2012 video was specially created by Alice Lemke ("Trip the Light" – available on iTunes). The mood and lyrics were a perfect accompaniment and included lines that celebrated the things that make us kin, no matter where we live, how we worship, or who we love.

Harding the family man has moved on to pursuits that do not require constant travel, but his videos are still regularly viewed and still attract donations for some of his favorite causes.

Loving "The Other"

You could hardly find two people more different from each other than Omar Khadr and Jack Hallam. Most people will recognize the former as the young man who threw a grenade during a 2002 firefight in Afghanistan, killing an American soldier. Hallman is a retired atheist.

Khadr was a 15-year-old boy in 2002, a Canadian citizen who experienced much of his childhood in Pakistan, his youth in Afghanistan, with a father who supported Al Qaeda. After his capture the young man spent a decade in the Guantanamo Bay detention camp. Although he was a minor at the time of the incident, he was charged with war crimes.

On September 29, 2012, he was repatriated to Canada to serve the last of his sentence. As an "unlawful combatant", Khadr was considered a criminal, and the country of his birth deemed him a terrorist.

Canadians were divided in their opinions about the young man, but an 84-year-old atheist wanted to help him out. Jack Hallam of Salt Spring Island was a retired zoologist, a gay man. He understood what it was like to be the object of stereotyping, suspicion and bullying, simply for being himself.

So Hallam wrote Khadr into his will, with a bequest of $700. He told the Canadian Press he was disturbed by the young man's harsh imprisonment. Kept in solitary confinement, subjected to torture, treated abominably, Khadr was, for Hallam, a young man being unjustly singled out for horrendous treatment.

Hallam was aware that a devout Muslim from an anti-West family might be surprised and even troubled by the gift. However, he believed Khadr deserved a chance to reintegrate into society.

Khadr's sentence ends in 2018. The small bequest from an unlikely stranger may seem a small gesture, given the enormity of venom heaped on Khadr since 2002, but it is one man's public refusal to accept another's cruel treatment.

Hallam's gift gives me hope that tolerance, forgiveness and compassion will win out, for Omar Khadr and all others caught in the crosshairs of political or social condemnation.

Our Flaws Are No Obstacles to Compassion

Aunt Grace held strong opinions on a lot of things. Sometimes she would say, "Don't be so open-minded your brains fall out." She meant you had to have moral fiber, that being open to others' ideas did not necessarily mean adopting their values and beliefs.

Aunt Grace had her flaws, but she was compassionate to her core. If someone knocked on the door at meal times, she would set another place and invite them in. That their politics or religious beliefs might be poles apart from her own had no bearing on her welcome nor her offers of assistance if they had fallen on hard times. She could be scrappy with her sisters and with people who disagreed with her, but she would do anything for them.

My aunt was the soul of generosity. She expected good things of people but did not turn her back on them when they failed to live up to her high hopes. I thought of her as I listened to Kristin Tippett's TED talk, "Reconnecting With Compassion".

Tippett says compassion is kind. It is curious. It can be synonymous with empathy and linked to generosity, hospitality, beauty and just showing up. But it is most assuredly not about being perfect.

She gives the example of Jean Vanier, who founded L'Arche. In that network of homes, people with developmental disabilities live in community with a handful of staff. She said of Vanier that he is not driven by a desire to change the world. Rather he is, as was as his friend Mother Teresa, driven by the wish to change himself.

Aunt Grace's sphere of influence was small by comparison with the people Tippett cites, but she was one of the most successful human beings I have ever met. She would probably have gotten along well with the notables Tippett mentions in her talk: Einstein, Gandhi, Martin Luther King, Jr., and Dorothy Day. They all had strong personalities. Put them in a room together, and they would likely have had some explosive conversations, but that would not have stopped them from making a mark on the world.

Tippett says they were all flawed, as are we all. She is right. Once we accept and embrace those flaws, we see they are as much a part of our humanity as are our freckles or blue eyes. They are fundamental to our humanity.

Our flaws are no obstacle to compassion. That makes me breathe a big sigh of relief, and it gives me hope.

Hope Starts at Home

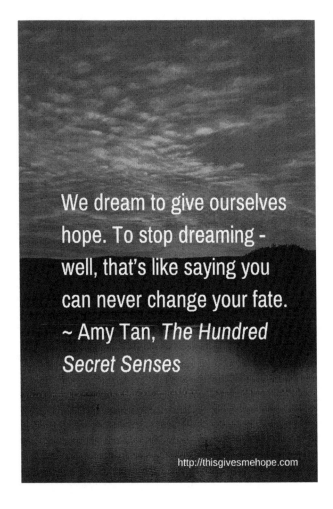

We dream to give ourselves hope. To stop dreaming - well, that's like saying you can never change your fate. ~ Amy Tan, *The Hundred Secret Senses*

Trouble Is What We Get; Life Is What We Do With It

Whatever our differences, we all have one thing in common: trouble.

The list of what can go wrong in our lives is probably finite. Everything on the list has been a bother to millions of us. Still, when it is our turn to fall off the mountain, we feel like the first to tumble to the bottom of that particular cliff. We do not know how to climb back up. We are alone and afraid.

When we hear, watch or read the experiences of survivors of a similar tumble, we feel stronger. We have a traveling companion who knows a piece of the road ahead, someone who can help us interpret that part of the map.

Trouble is always ahead, and it is always behind. So is joy. It is the colorful interweaving of both that gives our lives texture.

So we might as well join the growing number of people adding to an enormous weaving of hope. Together we can create patterns that lay a cloak of possibility over our mountain of troubles.

We can focus on the positive without ignoring the negative. By celebrating the best in each other instead of the worst, we can become a mighty force for change.

Buddha is often quoted as having said, "The mind is everything. What you think you become." And one of the most popular quotes attributed to Jesus is, "Ask, and it shall be given you; seek, and ye shall find; knock, and it shall be opened unto you."

That is timeless wisdom for us to tap into. We may be seen as cockeyed optimists, but the alternative is despair. And maybe, just maybe, our hope will go viral and transform the world, starting with ourselves.

We Can Change

Mother used to tell me I hit the terrible twos with a vengeance. My newly found power to manipulate the people around me was heady stuff for my small self. Adult-imposed limits became barriers to knock down. I reveled in the power to make grownups uncomfortable with my small rebellions.

As a single parent working five and a half days a week, Mother reached the end of her patience and finally hit on a technique that worked. On a day when I was playing happily and not testing any limits, she sat me down for a talk.

"You have to decide," she told me, "whether you are going to be a good girl or a bad girl. If you are a good girl, people will like you. They will want to play with you. They will trust you and let you do more things. If you are a bad girl, they will be angry with you a lot. They will not let you touch or play with nice things. You will be alone and unhappy.

"Which do you want to be? A good girl or a bad girl?"

I wouldn't answer.

When Mother told the story, she always said I pondered the question for three agonizing weeks. I'm not sure they were agonizing for me, but they were for my worried parent. Then one day, out of the blue, I said to her, "I've decided to be a good girl."

Decision made, I kept my word. Naturally I still occasionally got into trouble, but I halted my automatic opposition to limits imposed by others. I relaxed. Mother relaxed. The adults who cared for me during the day relaxed. Choosing to be good had benefits.

I am sitting at my computer on a snowy day, thinking about how our simple decisions can change a lot of the things that hamper us and harm our planet. We can decide to consume less so as to lessen our demands on the environment. We can decide to pay our fair share of taxes so the gap between rich and poor narrows. We can decide to show compassion to those who are suffering. We can decide to spend our dollars on food that is grown with respect for the earth. We can decide to stop stereotyping people whose culture, gender or social status are different from our own. We can decide to listen to each other with open hearts.

The list has no end, but it all boils down to our willingness to make decisions for the common good instead of just for our own self-interest. That sounds simplistic, and if it were easy we would be living in a perfect world.

Choosing to act for the common good is not a one-time decision. We fail at it miserably, time and time again. But when we take small and large steps in that direction, our efforts ripple outward.

A Circle of Love

I grew up with a single parent back in the days when such family configurations were uncommon. To keep a roof over our heads, Mother worked five and a half days a week for a seed company in Twin Falls, Idaho. We would have had a hard time surviving on her meager salary, but she gathered the proverbial village to help rear her two children.

Her oldest sister, Grace, and her brother-in-law, Dewey, would have been quite happy to feed us every day of the week. Aunt Grace loved to cook. Uncle Dewey enjoyed company. Aunt Grace sewed most of my clothes. Uncle Dewey slipped us a fiver when we were heading off to camp, always with the admonition: "Don't tell your mother."

Next door to them were Grandma and Grandpa Matthews. They were connected by love rather than blood and often looked after us when our "real" relatives were working. The Childress family lived nearby. They were another of the families that loved us best of all, along with any other children who came their way.

At the end of our street was Paul Friend, a sharecropper who filled our arms with melons and our ears with stories. Other neighbors and friends and cousins were an extended family.

They were our circle of love. We never had to earn their approval nor fear losing it. They kept an eye on us, listened to us, and encouraged us. They probably warned and occasionally chided us, but what I remember is the love. Lots of it.

Those loving adults did not have easy lives. Wealth and security were never on the horizon. What they had was big hearts, and that was more than enough to form a circle of love around us.

A Loving Generosity

Sun and earth are incredibly generous. Too often we respond by despoiling the planet. How different things would be if our connections with the earth and each other were characterized by largesse and acceptance.

So in the spirit of trying to keep hammering the lesson into my own head, I share these three photographs.

Each year the hills beyond my home are sprinkled with yellow flowers. We call the arrowleaf balsamroot our "Okanagan sunflower". They are miniature suns, reflecting back that star's rays. Their stay is short, but their impact on our sense of place lasts the year around.

Near our home the Rotary Club has created a small wildlife sanctuary to which this Great Blue Heron comes to fish. He is a study in mindfulness, fully present, absolutely still until he bends down to snatch a fish. Knowing he is safe, he ignores the humans watching.

The last photo shows the result of my partner's first attempt at making lasagna. It was a delicious success. Robin's cooking skills have blossomed in our time together. He keeps deciding he wants to master some dish he likes: lasagna, risotto, scalloped potatoes, a wide variety of soups.

I include the photo because Robin is one of those people who don't keep score. When he does something for me, he doesn't add it to a list to see if our contributions to the relationship are balanced. His is a generous heart, the kind we need more of in the world.

These are just three of the thousands of gifts I am given every day. They give me hope and remind me to end each day in gratitude.

Love's Sweet Honey

OK, I confess. My romance record is fractured. But I still believe in love. So does my sweet partner. We are a couple of old fogies who met when we were already used goods, but that does not take the shine off our sense of wonder at finding each other.

Years ago, while I was still in my first marriage (I have had two and am grateful for both), I made a flip comment to a friend. He was on his way to a friend's wedding. It was the third time around for both bride and groom.

"Well that's the triumph of optimism over realism," I snapped.

My friend grew quiet. "I've been married four times," he said, "but I still believe in love."

That friend was on his fifth marriage when he died. It was a solid, beautiful marriage. His four earlier marriages gave him happy memories. They foundered, it's true, but he did not consider them—or himself— failures because they ended.

Life is too short to bury it in guilt or regrets. Love is a gift. It does not matter how many times it is treasured nor how many times it ends. My Aunt Alice married six times. (One man she married twice because she could not live with him…or without him.) She died happy and fulfilled.

The couples in The Weepies' video of their sweet song, "Be My Honey Pie", may have come together just for the film. It does not matter. They are straight and gay, old and young. They represent the soul-deep need, the heart-full beauty of love. I get a bit weepy myself, watching them dance, kiss, love.

They embody love. I downloaded the song and sing it as I walk along. It is a reminder that as long as we are alive, we can hope, whether that hope is for a new partner or a visit with friends or even a peaceful world.

Everything starts with love in some way or another. And hope depends on our love's being stronger than our fears and doubts.

The Kindness of Strangers

I can still feel the skin scraping off my knees, shins, hands and arms as I skidded down the rough asphalt of the bike path. I can see the forest to my left, the highway to my right, the sun overhead, and the blood. I can recall the intense pain, as if the flesh had been burned off my bones.

My husband and I were living in southern Germany and had gone for a bike ride in the countryside near our home. I had tied a daypack onto the rack behind my seat. At the top of a steep hill, I felt the pack slip to the left.

The bike picked up speed. The shifting pack sent it off balance. I reached back to center it on the rack. The bike skidded out from under me, and I began a long slide down the hill.

Shock delayed the excruciating pain. What happened next gave me hope. The first driver to see me fall stopped. So did every other driver who passed on that country road.

It was the spring of 1981, before the era of cell phones. The driver of the first car went off to find the

74

nearest home so he could call an ambulance. Others put jackets under my head, to lift it off the pavement. Some shaded me from the sun. They spoke softly, moved quietly, and assured me they would not leave until help arrived.

I do not remember how many were there when the ambulance arrived, but as soon as they knew I was in good hands, they continued on their way.

A rural clinic was not far away. The doctor cleaned my wounds as gently as he could. He was quiet and reassuring, as the passersby had been.

Though the intense pain lasted only a few weeks, healing took a long time. That fall I began work as a primary school librarian. The children who gathered at my knees would touch the scars and ask me to tell the story again and again

I still have the scars. They are reminders of the kindness of strangers, who interrupted their journeys to look after me. They confirmed what so many others did in that year of being an American in Germany. Good people can be found everywhere.

Every Child Needs a Paul Friend

The tiny house my single mother could afford was on Jackson Street, in Twin Falls, Idaho. At the time, it was a dead-end street.

At its end lived a sharecropper, Paul Friend. Children always figure out who lives in a neighborhood long before their parents do. I don't remember how my brother and I first introduced ourselves to Paul Friend, but we soon learned he grew the sweetest cantaloupe and the juiciest watermelon we had ever tasted.

In my mind's eye is a vivid picture of his spare frame, clad in overalls and a dark blue work shirt, bent over the rows of melons he lovingly tended. Now and then he would stop for a break. He would pull out a pocketknife, open the blade, and slice into a perfectly ripe melon.

He would pass slices to his young visitors, and we would sit in the field, juice running down our arms. All was right in our world when we were with Paul Friend. He didn't talk much, but he listened a lot, with the kind of attention that pulls the best out of us at any age.

When he first sent us home with our arms loaded with melons, Mother marched down to his small farm.

Melons were a treat we could rarely afford, but she was not going to allow us to take advantage of our new friend. If we accepted melons, we had to pay for them.

He understood how hard she was trying to bring us up with good values. So now and then he would take a nickel or a dime, just to keep things straight with Mother.

But money was never the real medium of exchange. What he offered with those melons was love, bushels of it along with the melons of our years on Jackson Street.

The 75/25 Rule

S teep trail ahead. Small group of hikers: Robin, me, a guide and two young men, all in their twenties, two more men in their late 40s. I was the only woman. Robin and I doubled the average age.

Since we were on a cruise ship sailing the Inside Passage, I figured this particular shore excursion would include plenty of us oldies. Somehow I overlooked the icon that showed this to be on the upper end of the easy-to-extreme scale.

The trip was scheduled at a time when Robin (who was on board as tour director for a group of Australians) could come with me. So I signed up for a two-hour hike on the famous Chilkoot Trail and a float back along the Taiya River.

On the drive to the trailhead, I fretted over how I would keep up. At the start of the trail, I contemplated the steep stretch ahead and wondered how I could gracefully opt out.

Like many personal mountains in life, this one turned out to be a molehill. Steep sections were short. Trail conditions were ideal. The group was congenial and kind. The guide stopped frequently.

The piles of fresh bear scat didn't worry me. I had lived around a bear family one summer and knew they preferred to avoid contact with humans.

By the time we reached the river and the rubber raft, we were a friendly group. When the skies opened, we donned the ponchos provided by Chilkat Guides, climbed in the yellow craft, and bobbed cheerfully down the river to the waiting hot chocolate. Water was high, near flood level, but the guide knew where all the boulders and snags were.

The outing turned out to be a highlight of our Alaska cruise. I didn't slow the group down, but I did give the young men a chance to demonstrate their kindness. All that pre-hike worry was exactly what my ex used to call the 75/25 rule: "75% of the things you worry about never happen."

I think of that rule when I fret about the Big Issues. We are, after all, not powerless in the face of challenges and adversity, not as individuals, not as humans. We can put our collective heads together and change things.

A Simple Path to Happiness

Life is both hard and easy. When someone says all we have to do is think positively and everything will be OK, I think about an Afghani woman beheaded for adultery. The idea that she just didn't think positively enough does not sit right with me.

Don't get me wrong. I know I'm my own worst enemy. I also know that attitude plays a huge role in our lives. Viktor Frankl taught me a lot about that in his book, *Man's Search for Meaning*. Patti Digh's *Life Is a Verb: 37 Days to Wake Up, Be Mindful, and Live Intentionally*, another favorite of mine, repeated the message in a different way.

I am not willing to concede that people get cancer, fail at business, suffer the suicide of a child or die in a plane crash simply because they do not have the right attitude or have chosen that particular life lesson. Still, a big dose of gratitude for what is right in our lives seems in order.

When I was going through a rough patch a while back, I stumbled onto the work of Martin Seligman. He is the founder of positive psychology. A lot of what he

80

had to say made sense to me and helped me shift my focus.

Even earlier, I found Hannah Hinchman's *A Life in Hand: Creating the Illuminated Journal.* She taught me to draw my days. Instead of of filling my journals with a litany of woes, I learned to capture the lift of a raven's wing and the fleeting color of a sunset.

Much later I came across Jamie Gruman, co-founder of the Canadian Positive Psychology Association. In an interview reported in the *Vancouver Sun,* he said, "We're trying to find out what makes people happy because we've learned it isn't money."

That is certainly true for me. Friends and loved ones, writing and photography, good food, and comfortable shoes make me happy. I don't need much more, though living surrounded with beauty, as I do now, makes me deeply grateful. That is the secret to happiness, mine anyway: gratitude. And gratitude is a solid building block for a foundation of hope.

We All Have a Right to Peace; Someone Must Begin

September 21st is the International Day of Peace (often called World Peace Day). Around the world vigils, prayers and parties bring people together to imagine a world in harmony. In communities, organizations, families and on their own, people are asked to focus on peace. It is a visible celebration of what John Lennon called for in his song, "Imagine".

The idea is that if we come together to focus on peace, personal or political, for one day, perhaps we can learn the peace habit. We may find it easier to believe peace is possible if for one day we cease all hostilities.

Everyone, everywhere has a right to peace. Too many political and religious organizations seem to figure peace is only for those who follow their ideologies. It is tempting to look around the globe and despair.

But David Orr has it right. He is a distinguished environmental educator at Oberlin College and the University of Vermont. In *Hope Is an Imperative* he writes that in spite of all the reasons for despair, he believes if

82

we persist, if we dream, if we act, we can free ourselves and our world from greed, hatred and maybe even from our propensity for destroying our planet and each other. For Orr hope is a challenge he is willing to take on.

We can imagine peace, imagine living in harmony with each other and the planet, imagine a world where social justice is everyone's birthright. And whatever we can imagine, we can make real. For such a radical transformation, Orr says we need champions. Some are obvious, like our politicians, business titans, public officials, educators and media. But all of us are needed, and Orr figures ordinary people will be at the forefront, you and I and others who say a loud "Enough" and change directions.

We can do this, Orr believes, and someone must step forward and start.

So let's begin. We can do this...together.

Catch the Hope Habit

A quote attributed to Rumi wryly claims that yesterday he was so smart he had ambitions to change the world. Today, with more wisdom than before, he is going to change himself.

I hear loud bells ringing when I read it. When I began to blog for This Gives Me Hope, I envisioned spreading a bit of hope around by keeping my inner sensors waving in the breeze to catch whiffs of it. Perhaps the hope would ease some of the stress of so much focus on the negative.

What I did not envision was the impact it would have on me. The more posts I wrote, the more I realized I was the one who needed the lessons.

My heart can be a tough nut. I see injustice and hop on the speaker's platform to rail against it. Canada's Conservative government and America's crazy right wingers send me into waves of self-righteous anger. Misogyny makes me want to take up a cudgel and start whacking away at the narrow-minded, blind fools who harbor it. Greed, environmental destruction…

See what I mean? I can go from calm and peaceful to fist shaking in less than a second. That is why I needed to start the search for reasons for hope. Months went by. Whenever I slipped into rant mode, all I had to do was surf around among the stories I was collecting and writing. Every time I did, I felt a surge of…well…HOPE.

We all need to cultivate a habit of hope. It is the only way to avoid falling into despair. Children deserve to grow up with hope. A quote from Elie Wiesel keeps running through my brain: "If dreams reflect the past, hope summons the future."

All you hope-filled people have given me so much encouragement I wrap you in hugs. You have sent ideas, links, support and e-mails that have brought tears to my eyes. You are the reason this hope journey is so joyous.

If you are new to this journey, welcome to the hope tribe. You give me hope.

About the author

Cathryn Wellner is a writer and photographer who can usually be found either staring at her computer screen or taking her camera for a walk. She is on a hunt for what is right with the world and blogs about the creative, generous, brilliant, kind, inventive people who are making a mark on the planet.

Most of her writing is online these days, but she is venturing back into the print world with the *Hope Wins* series and a forthcoming memoir, *The Reluctant Farmer* (http://thereluctantfarmer.com).

Contact her at cathryn@cathrynwellner.com, on Twitter (@StoryRoute), Facebook (at This Gives Me Hope) or via her Web site, This Gives Me Hope. She can also be reached at 778-478-2760.

Thanks & a request

Readers are the best kinds of people. Book buyers are in the angel category. Your purchase of this book helps keep the hope coming. It is available in digital and print versions. If you bought the print version, send a copy of your receipt to cathryn@cathrynwellner.com, and I will send you a free copy of the PDF e-book, which has all kinds of hyperlinks embedded in it, as well as many more photographs.

If you enjoyed this first book in the Hope Wins series, please post a review on Goodreads or Amazon or iTunes. Send a copy of your review to cathryn@cathrynwellner.com to receive the next e-book (PDF format) in the series free.

Excerpts from Amazon reviews:

"'Hope Wins' shows the way to shedding a cynical view of life, by providing numerous examples where the 'good' in people were expressed and shared." ~ Amazon Customer

"A master storyteller and writer, Cathryn Wellner brings us pieces that truly inspire and bring joy, crafted with excellent prose." ~ lkw

"Life always offers hope Wonderful stories to help the spirit soar as only a master story teller Cathryn Wellner can deliver." ~ Teresa Myszka

Made in the USA
Charleston, SC
16 September 2015